Gothic Inspiration

grayscale cloring book

curated by

Tabz Jones

FIRST EDITION 2016

TABZ JONES
PO BOX 2137
ALMA, AR. 72921
WWW.GOTHICTOGGS.NET

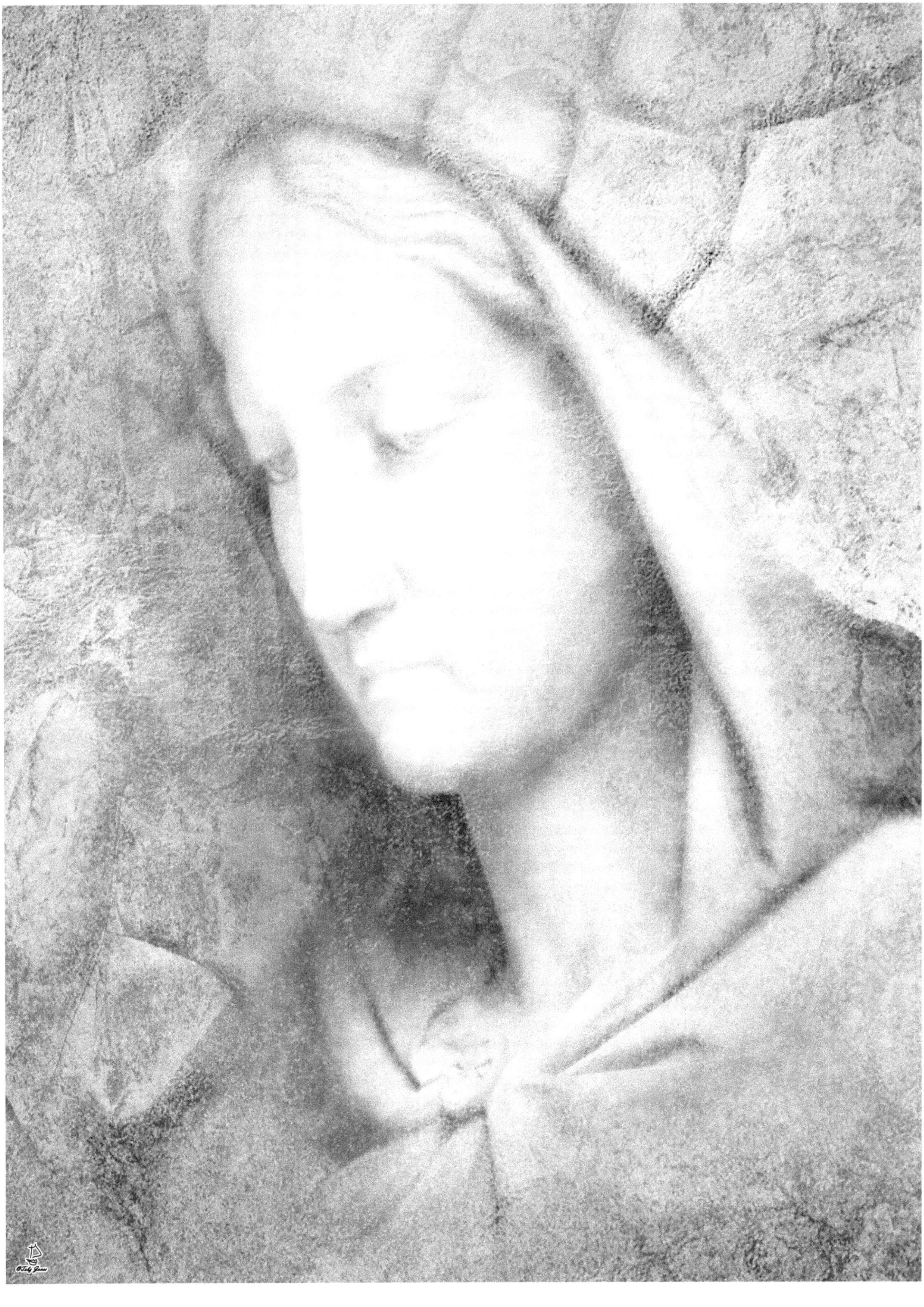

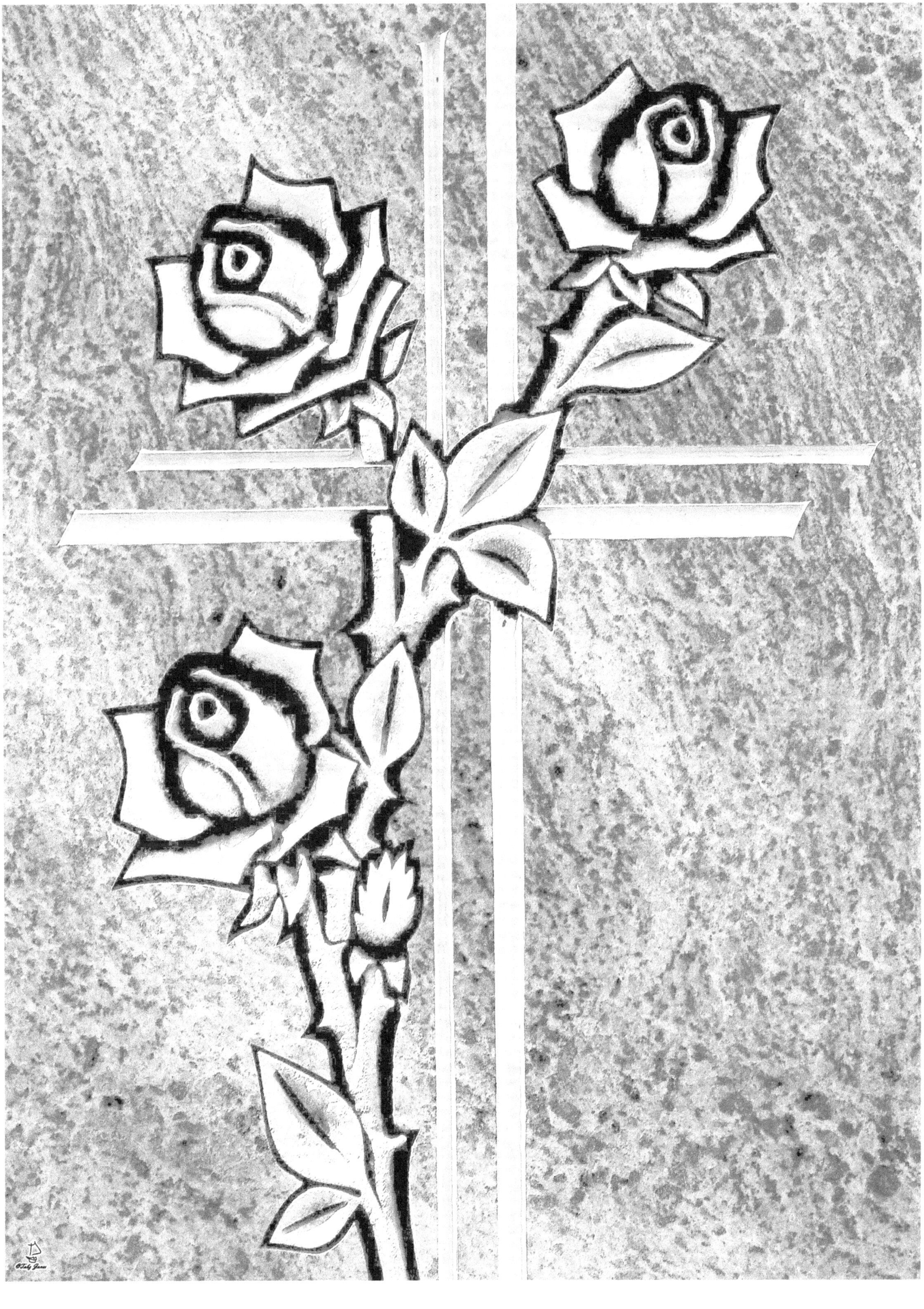

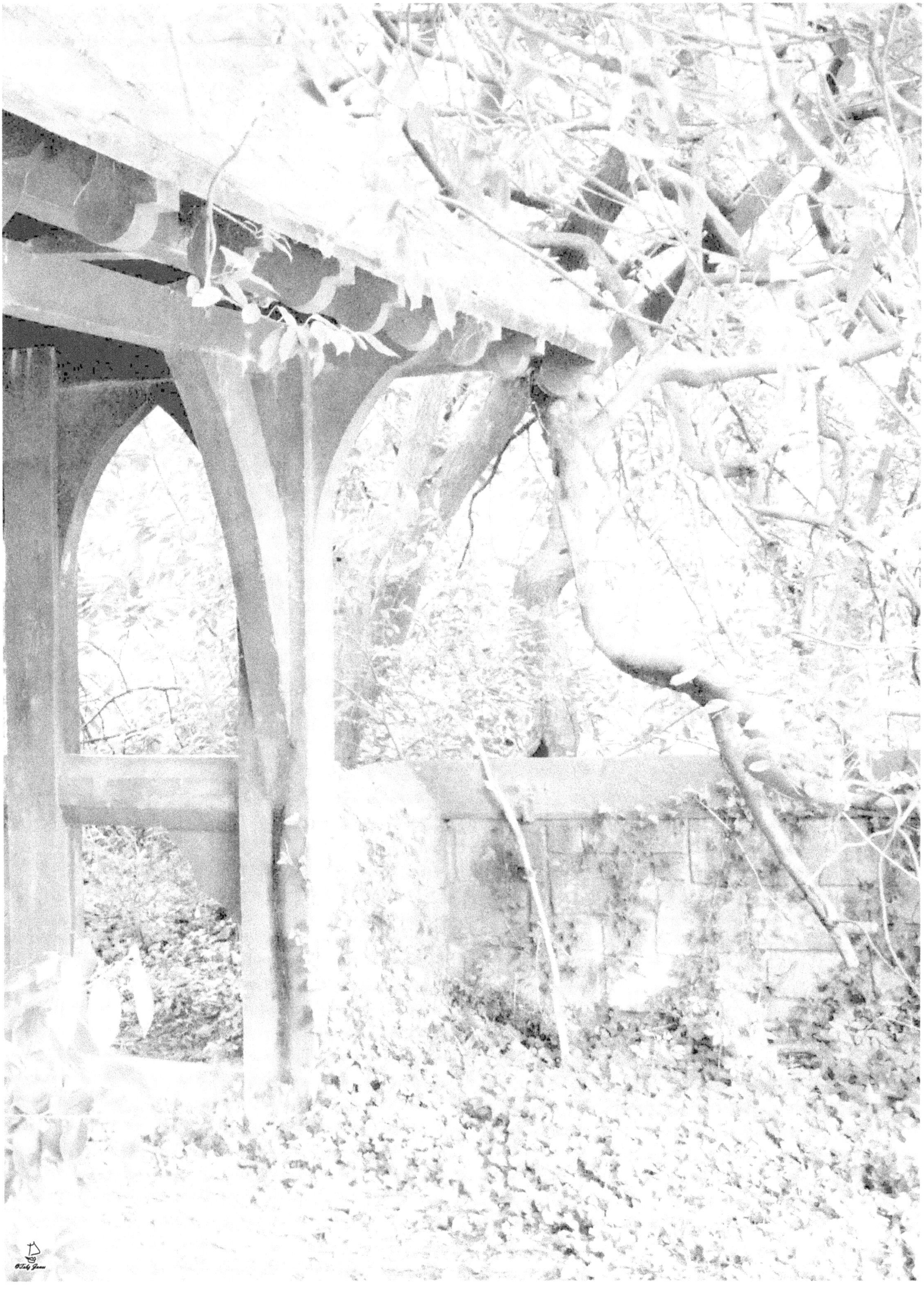

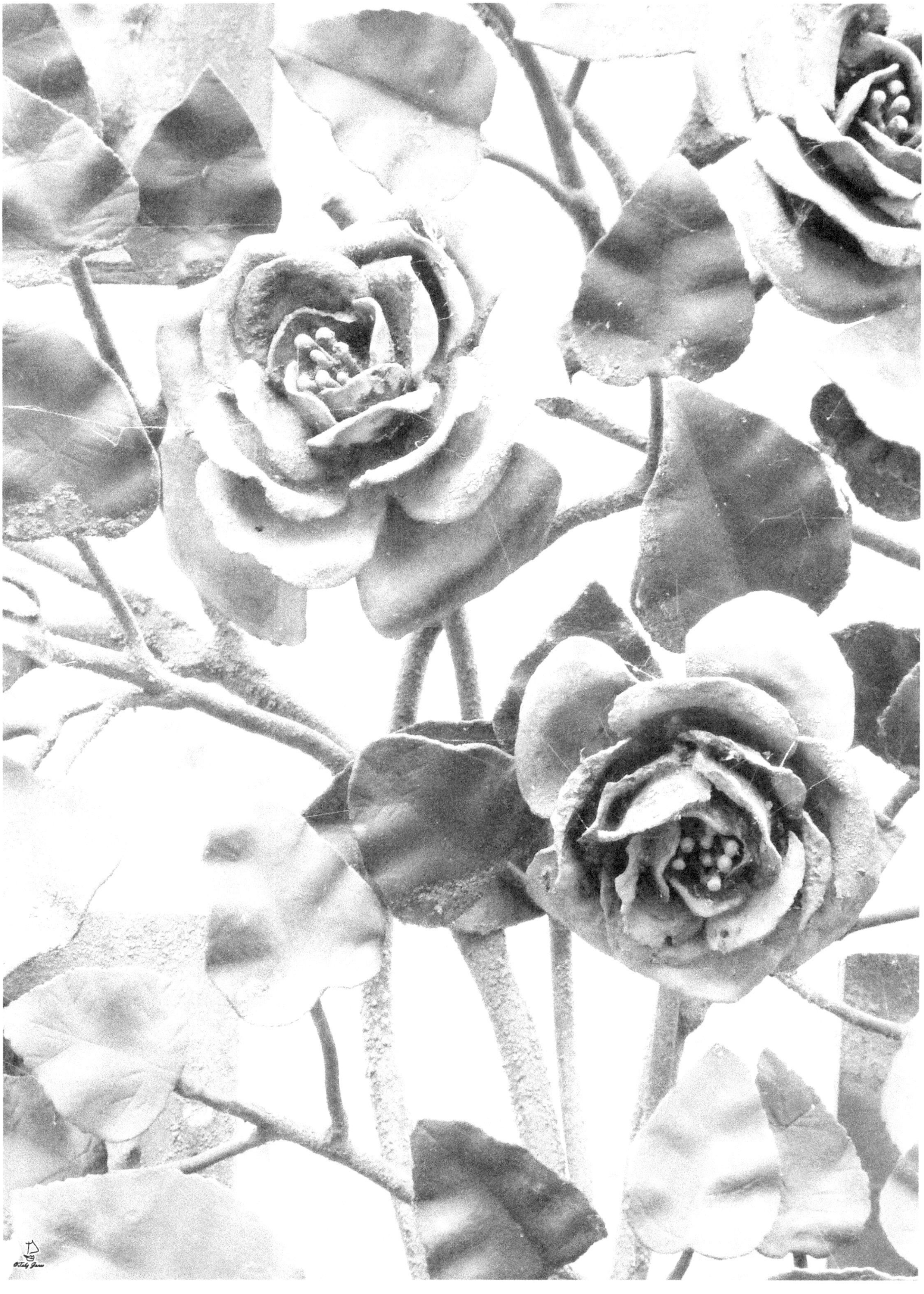

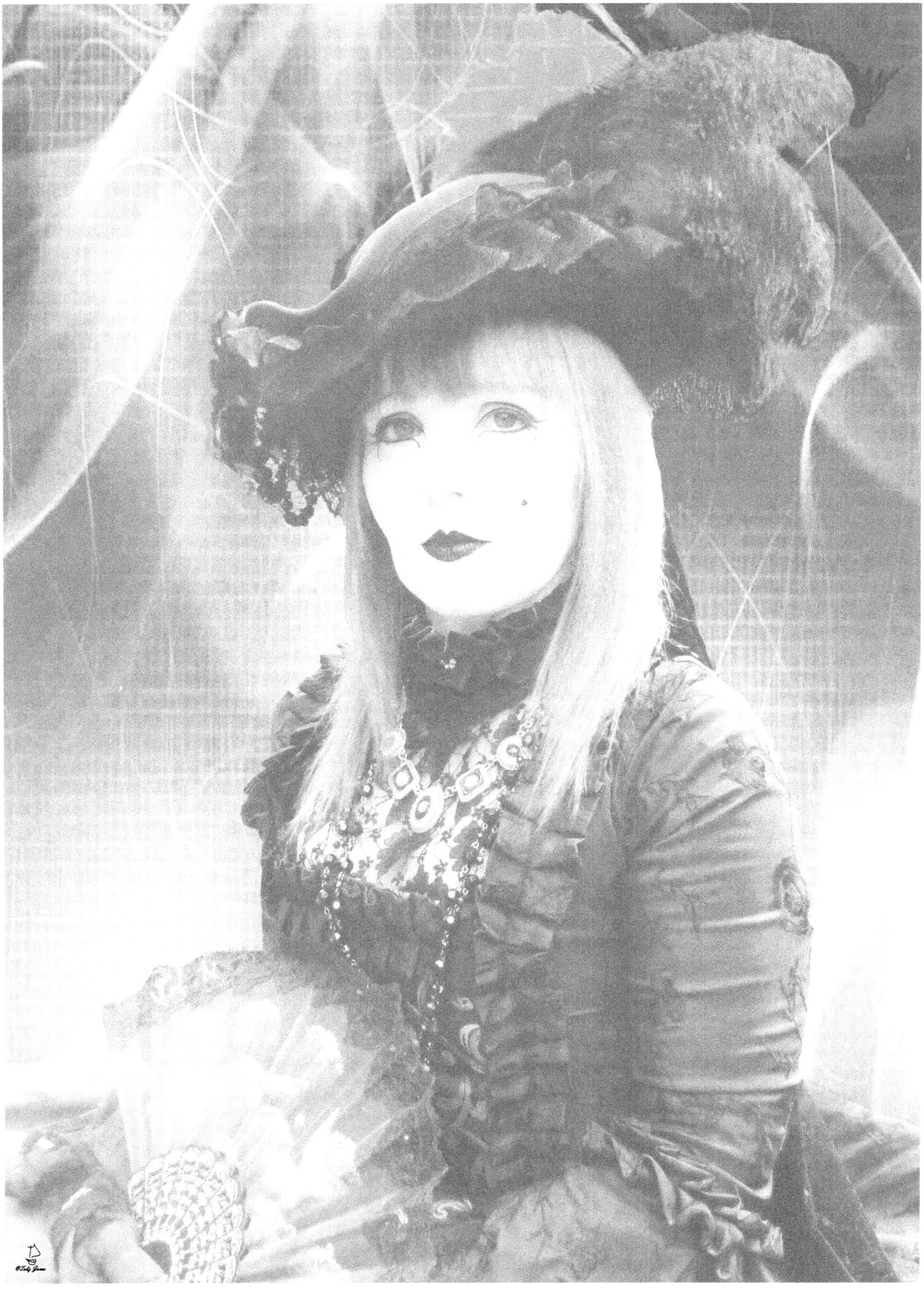

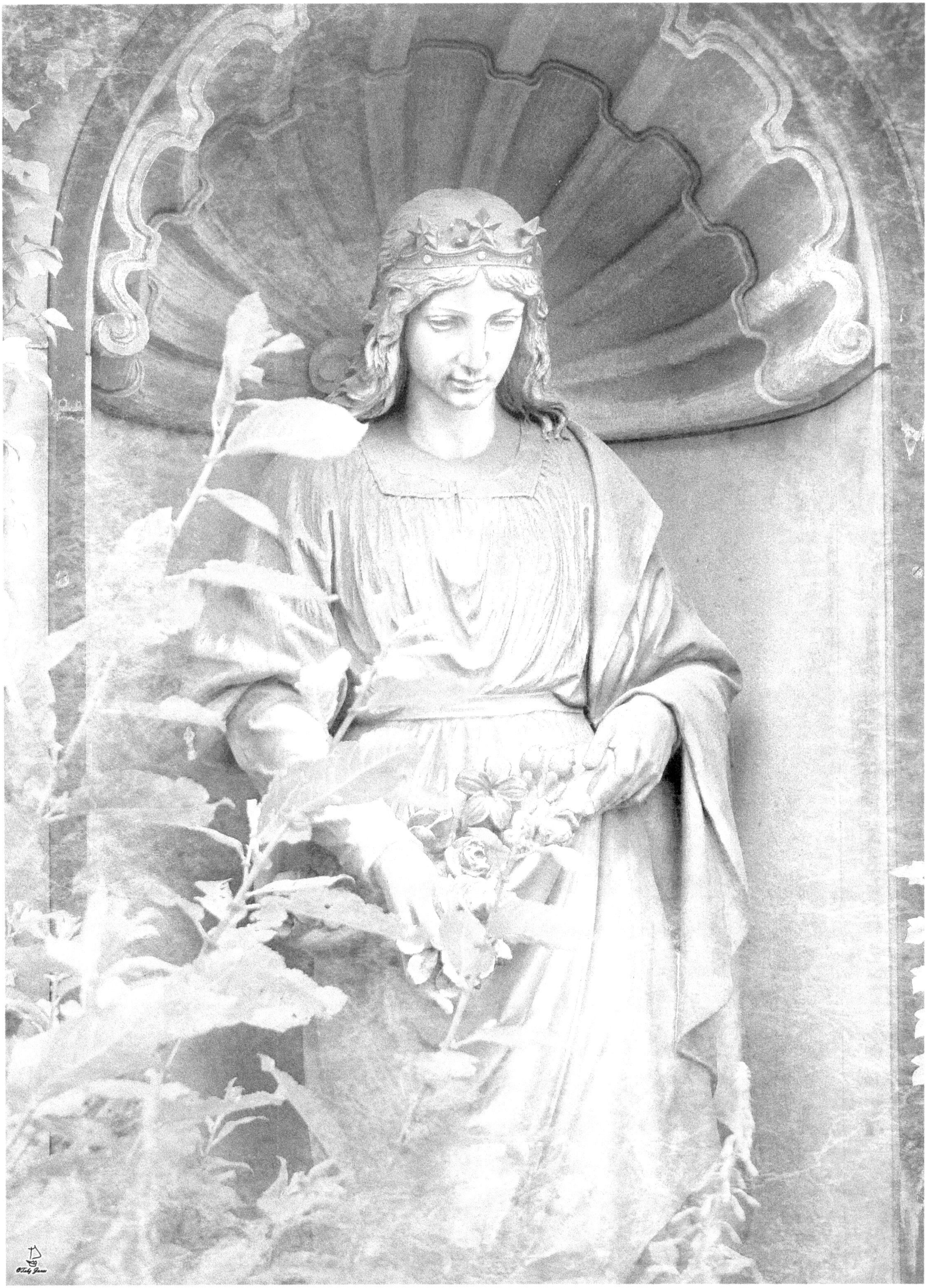

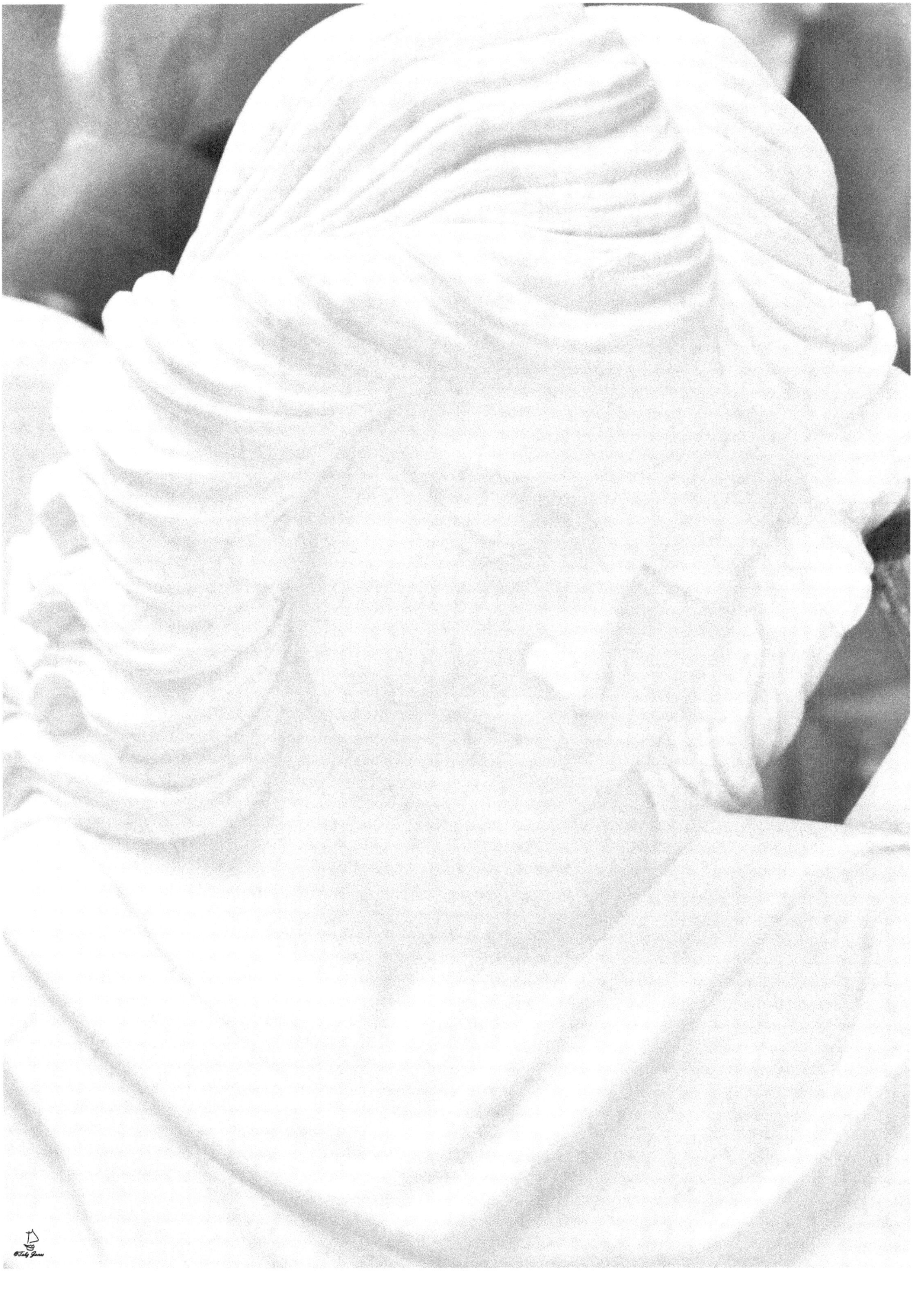
©Toby James

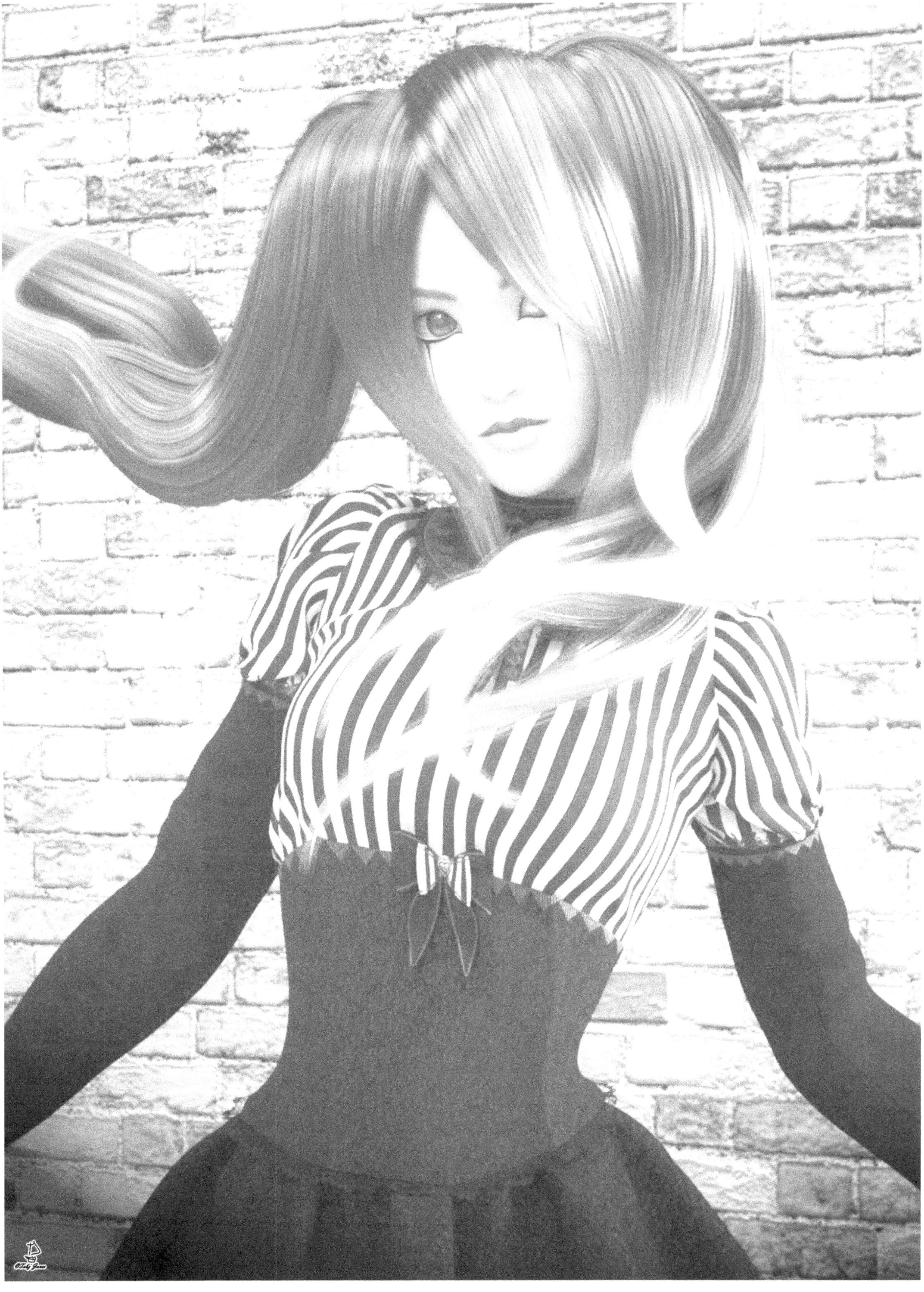

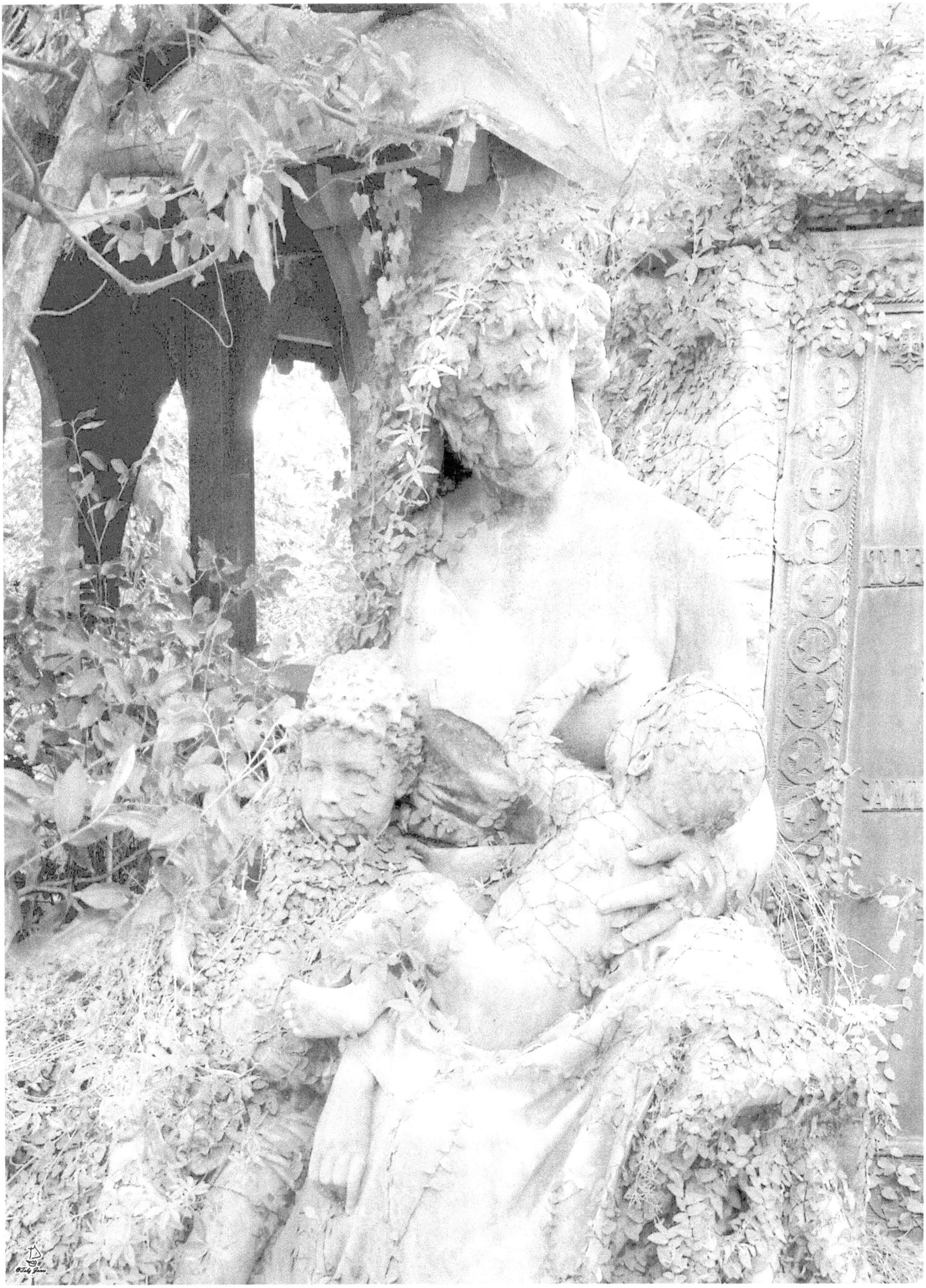

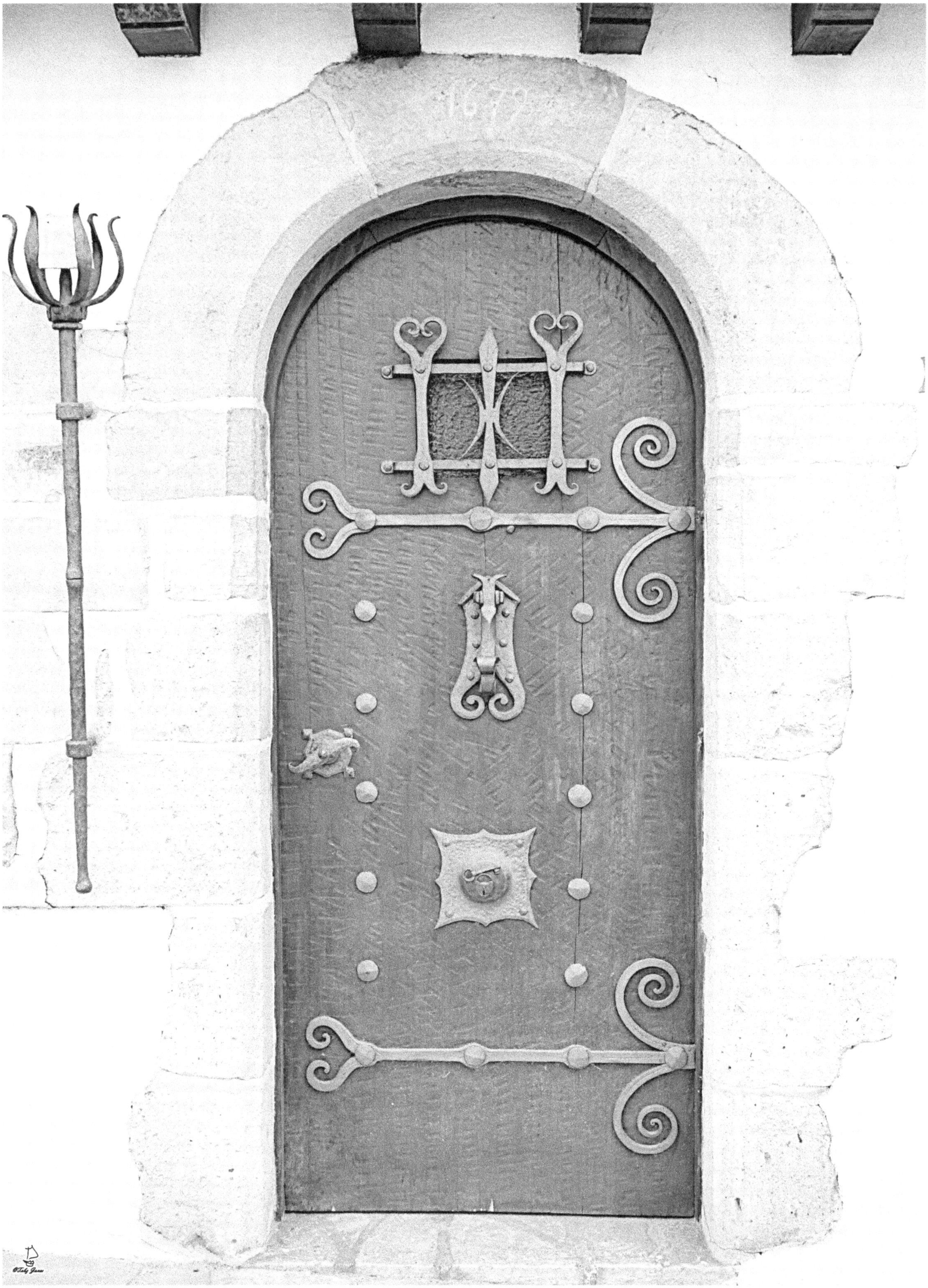

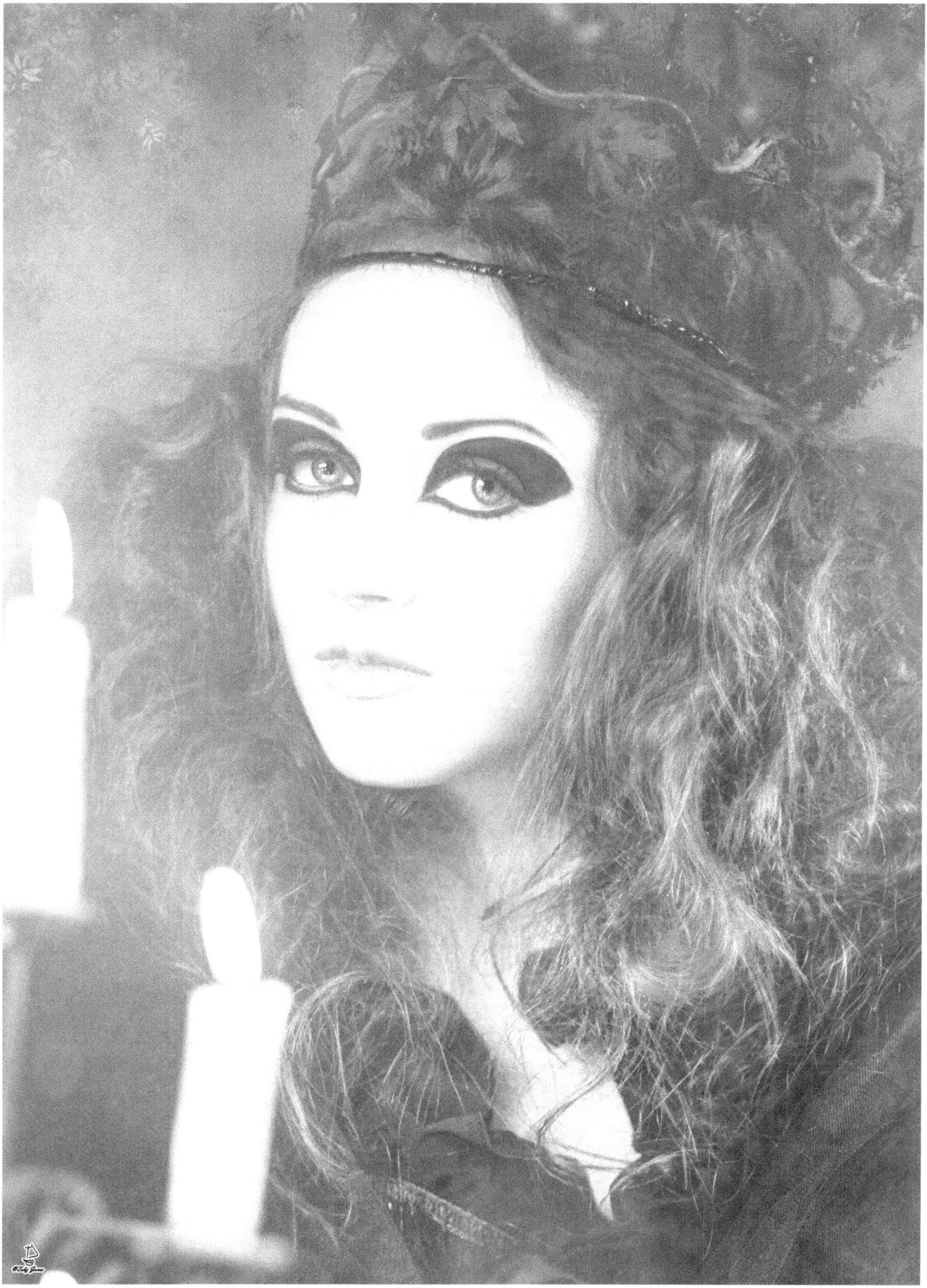

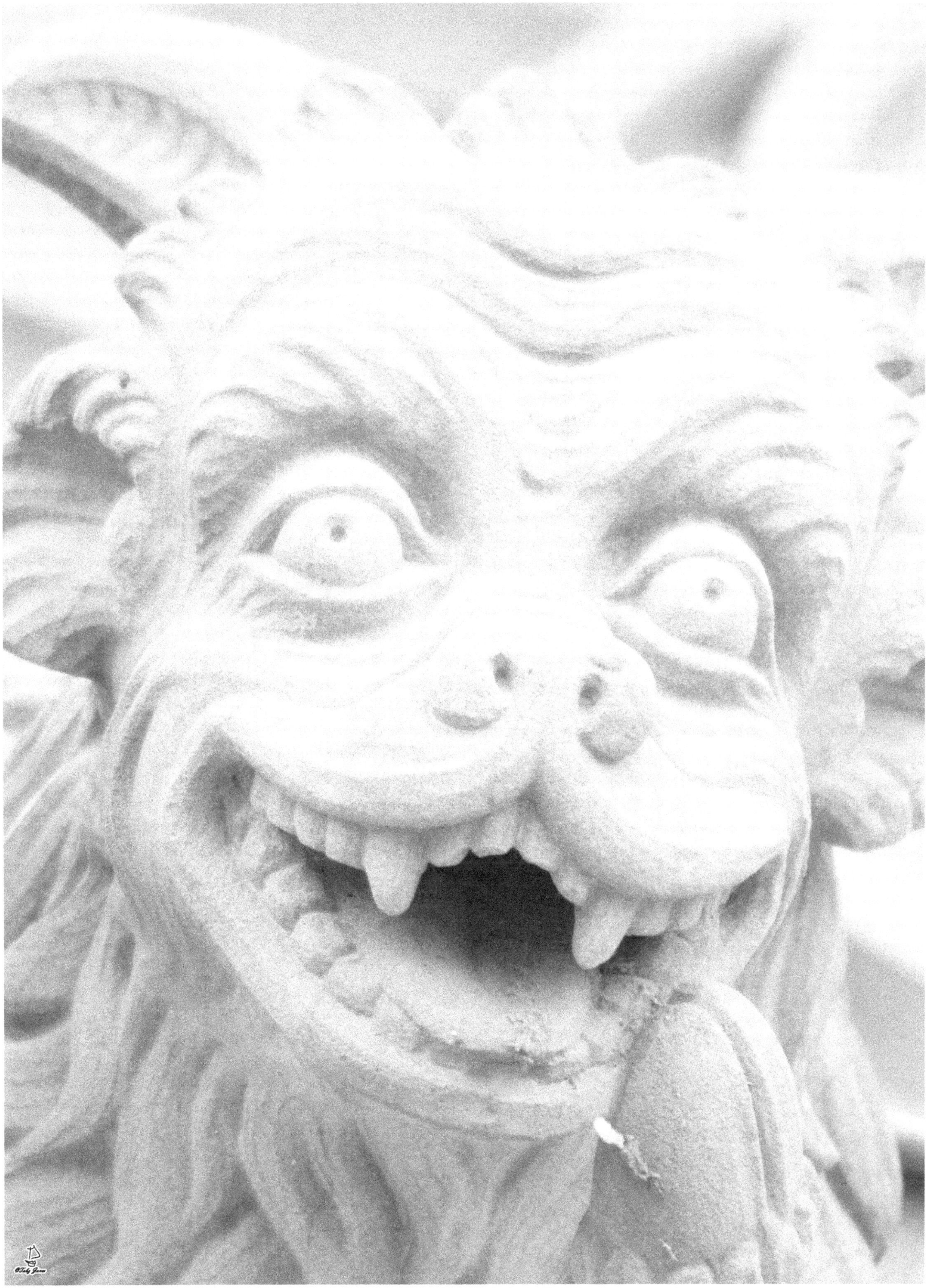

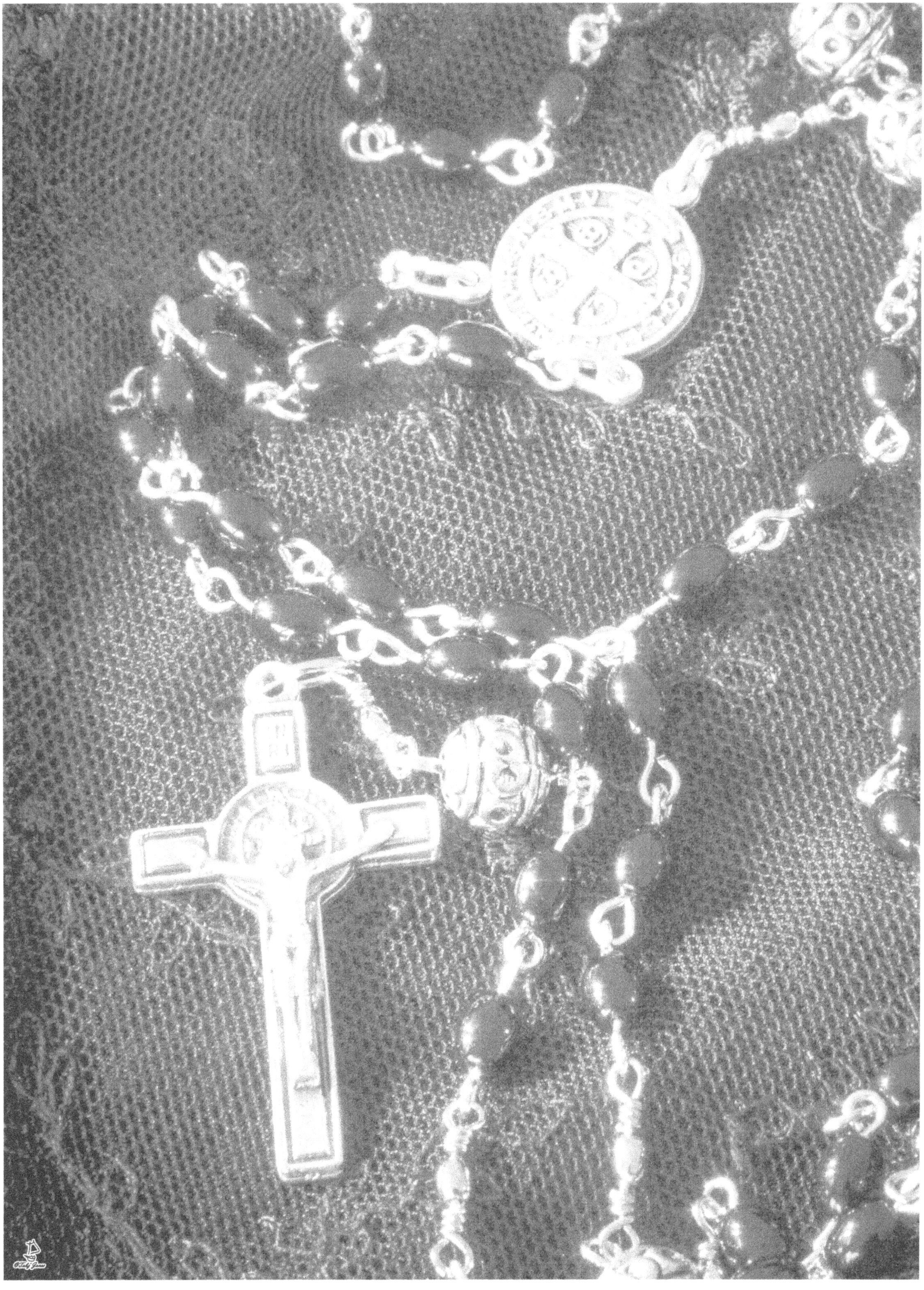

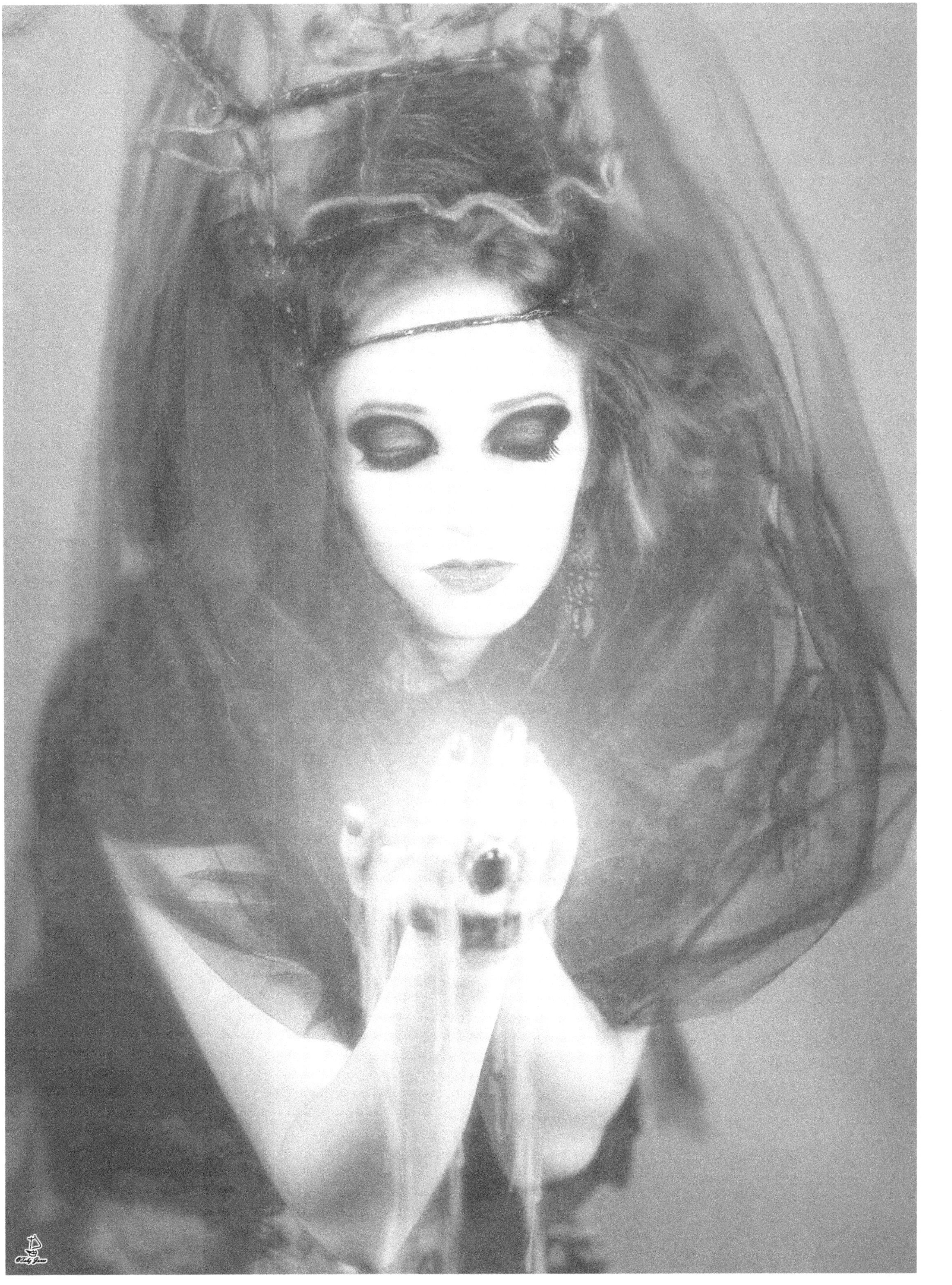

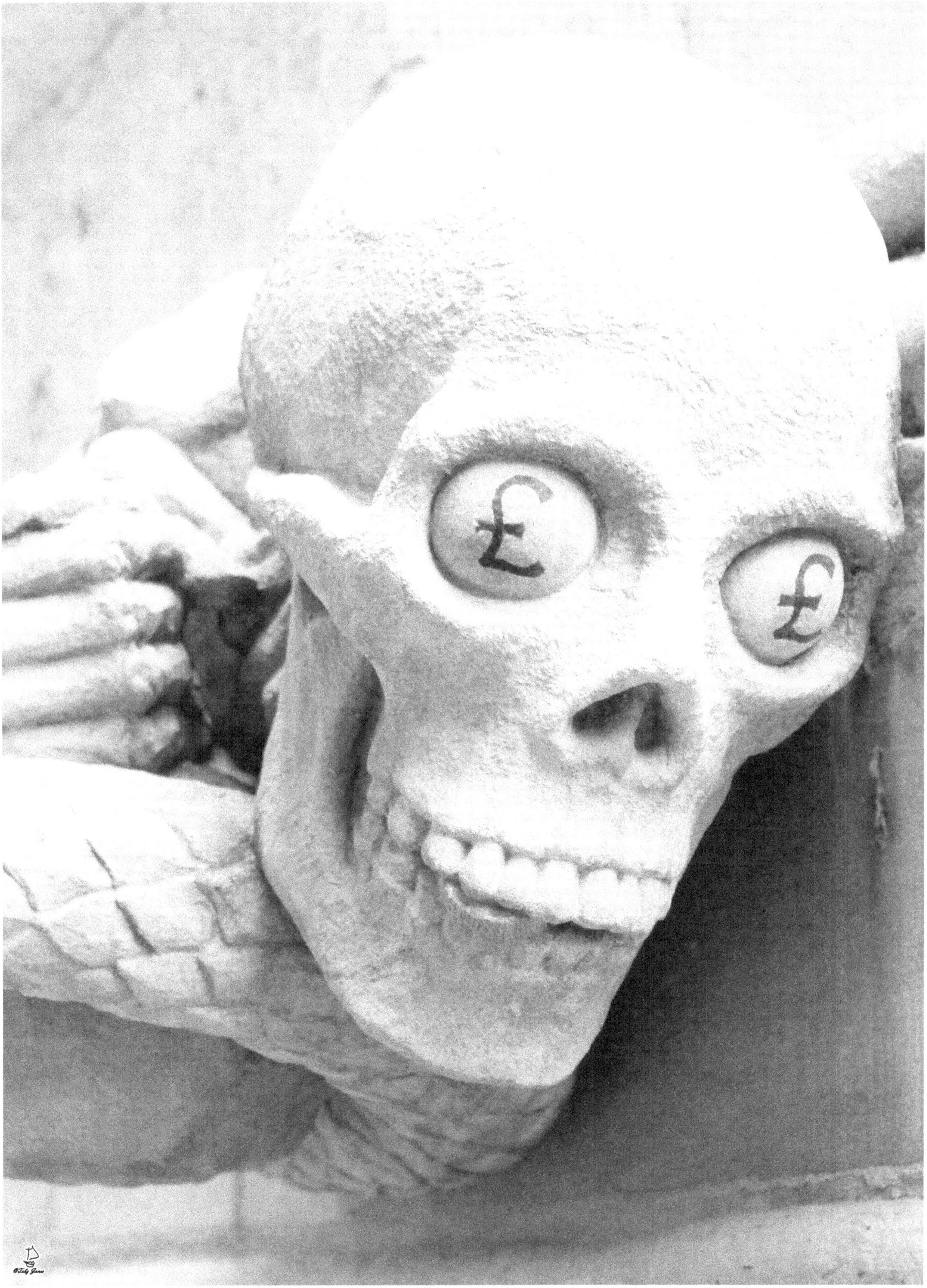
©Toby Jones

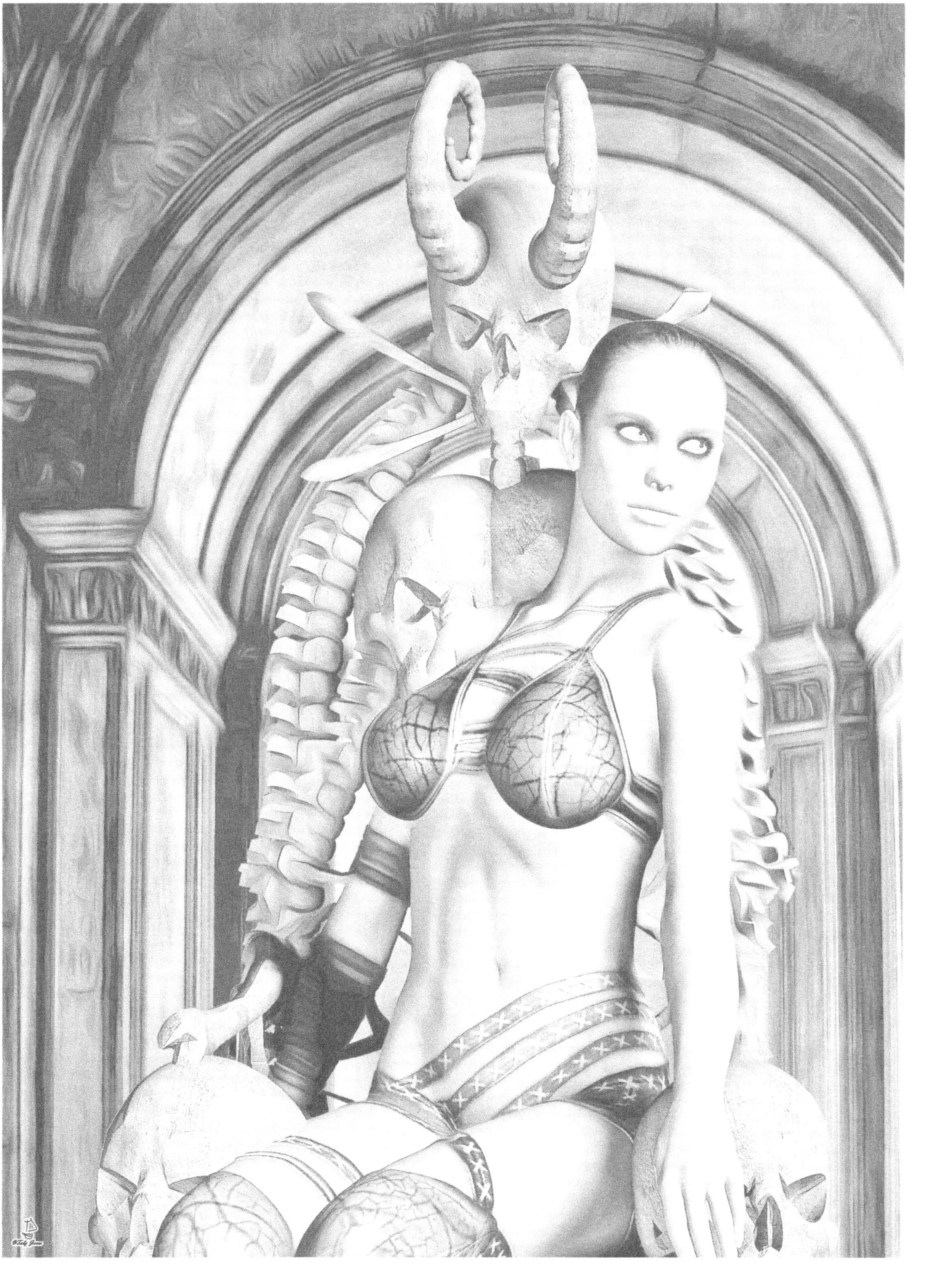

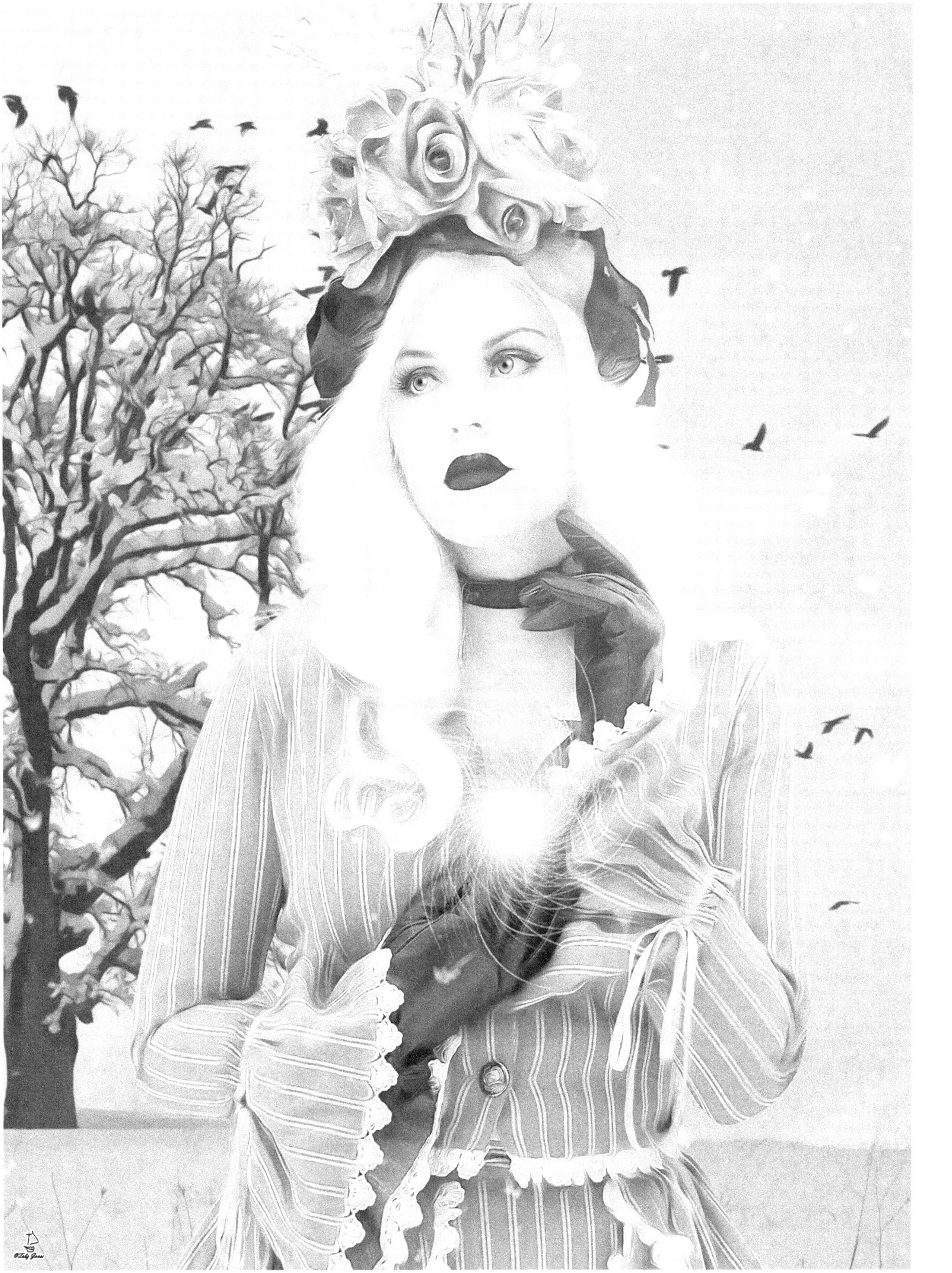

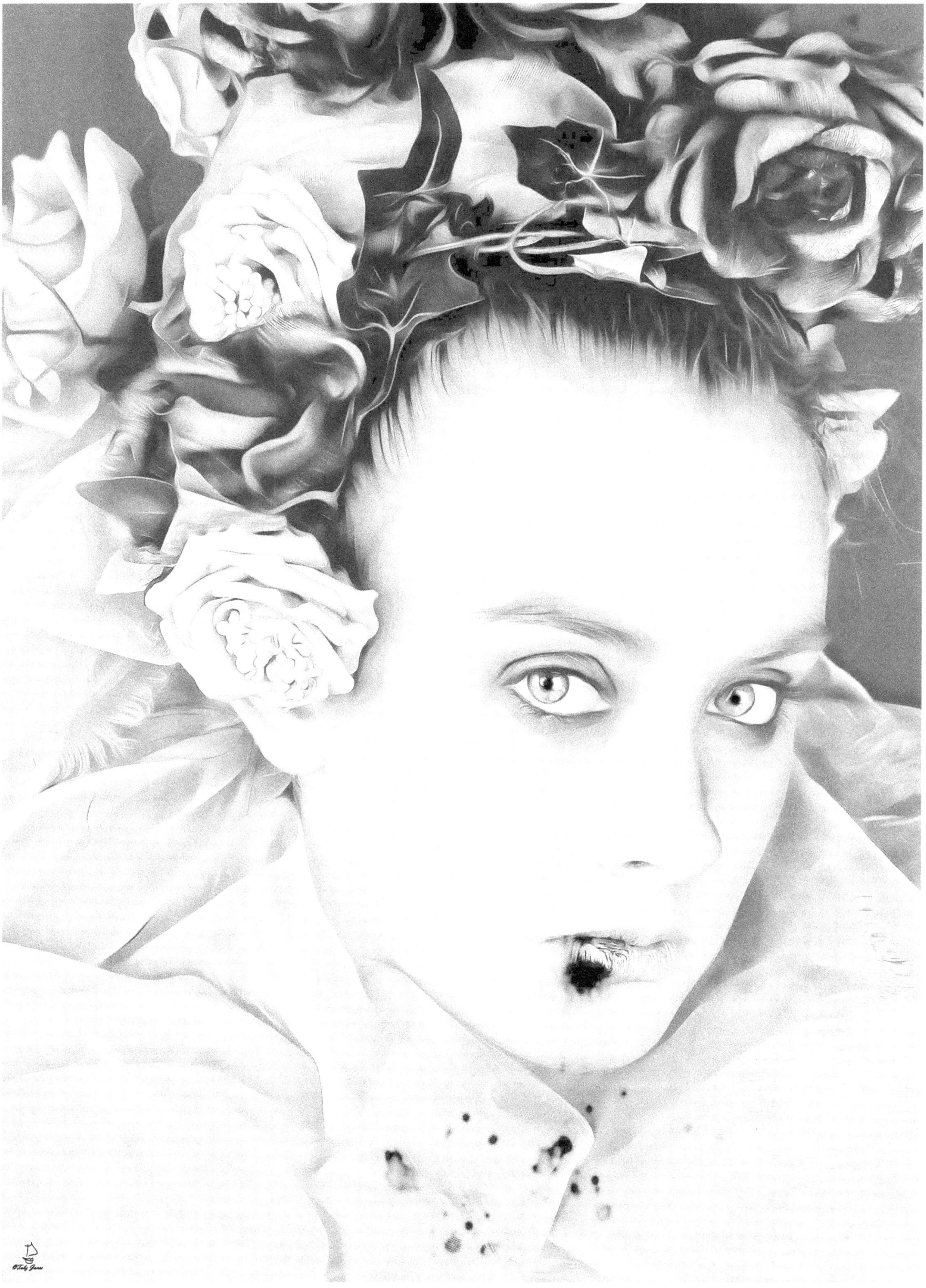

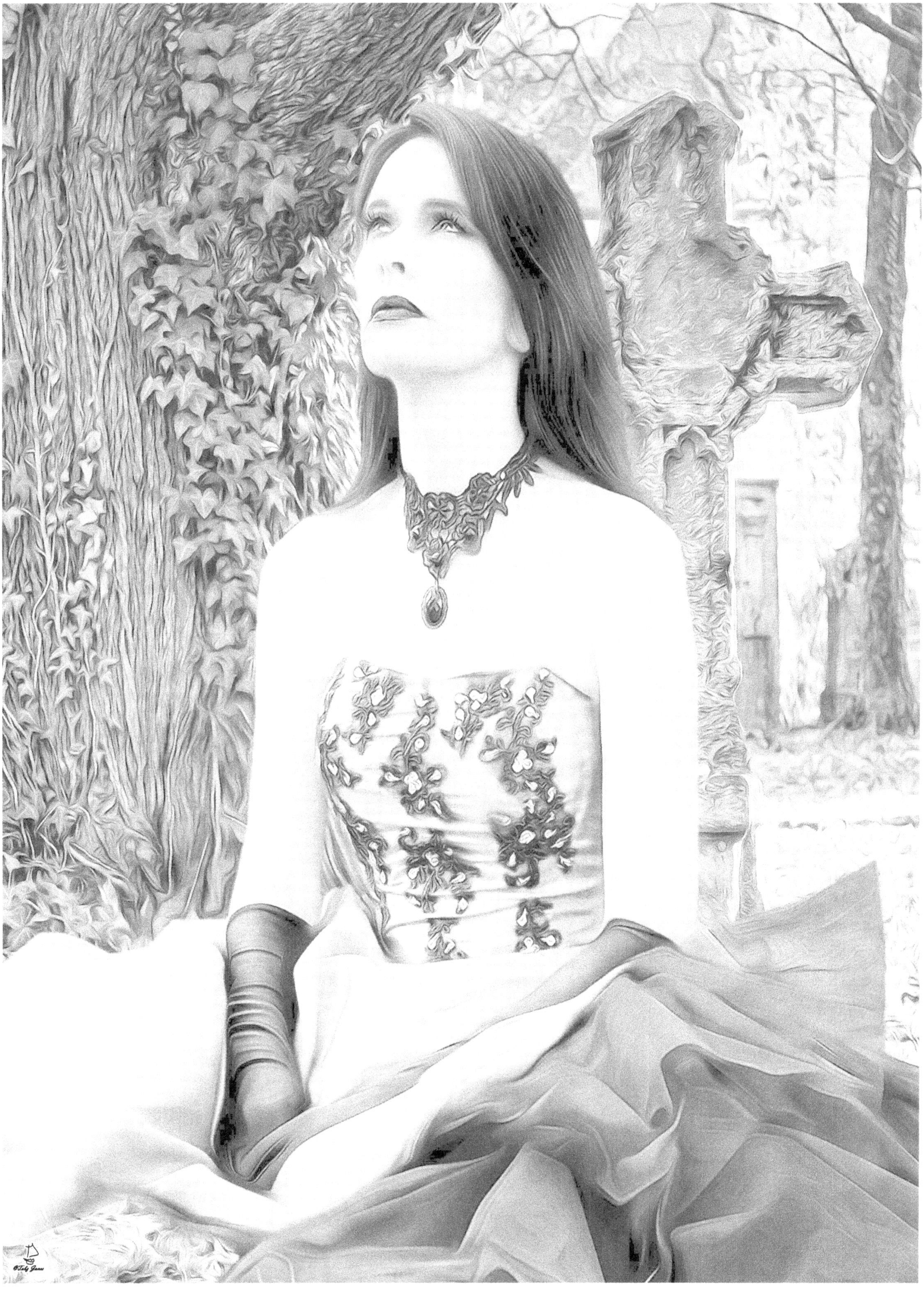

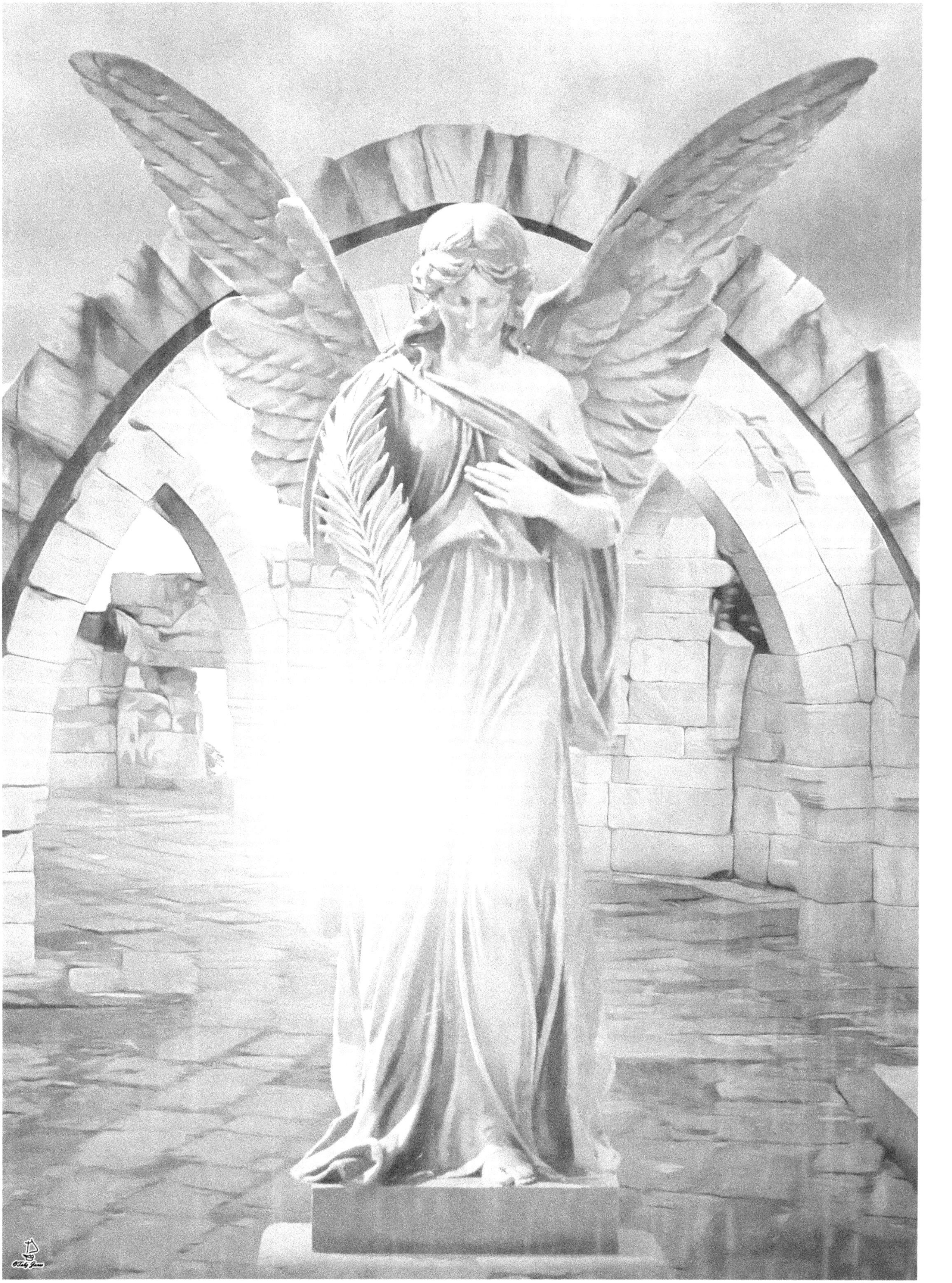

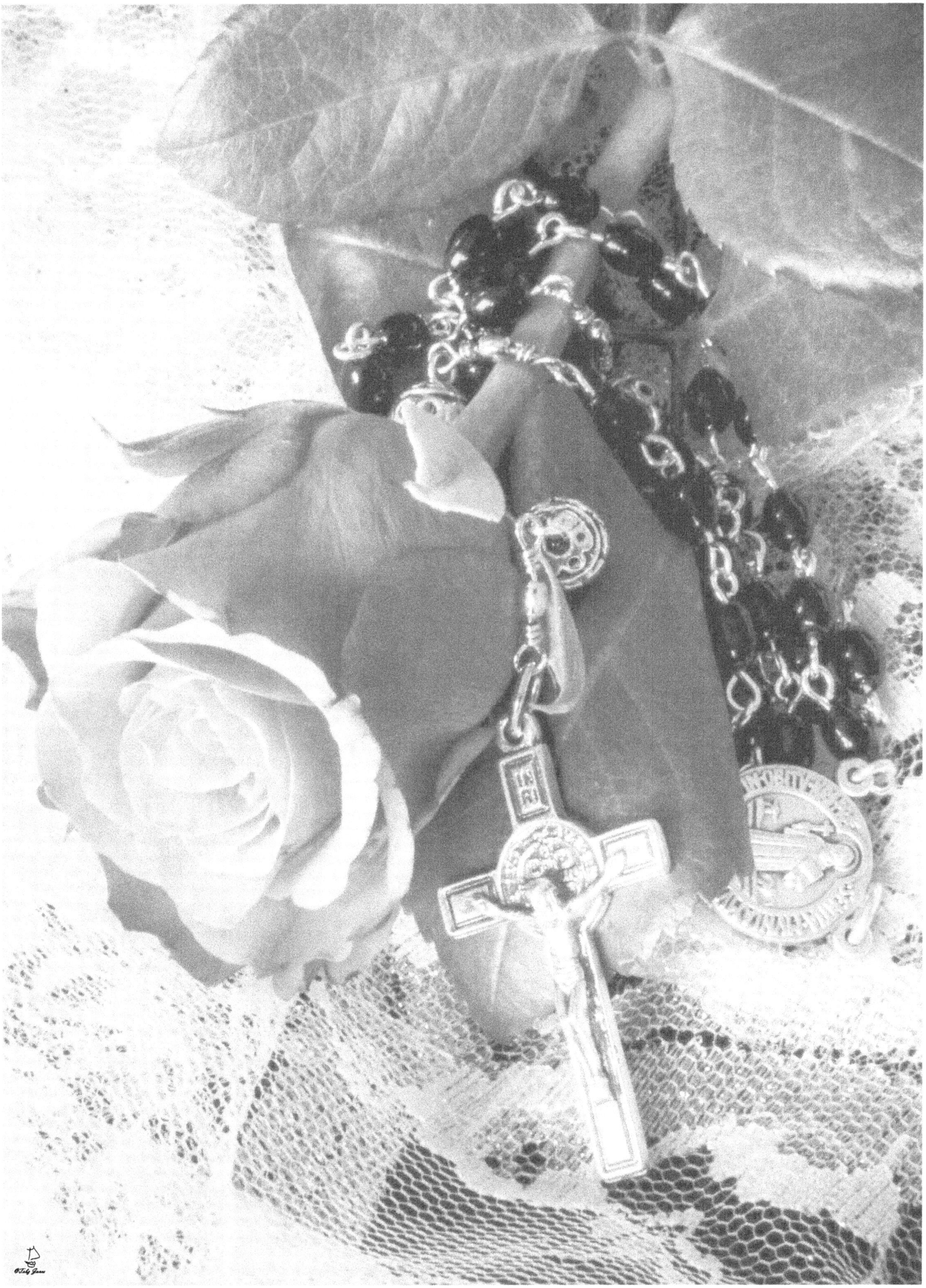

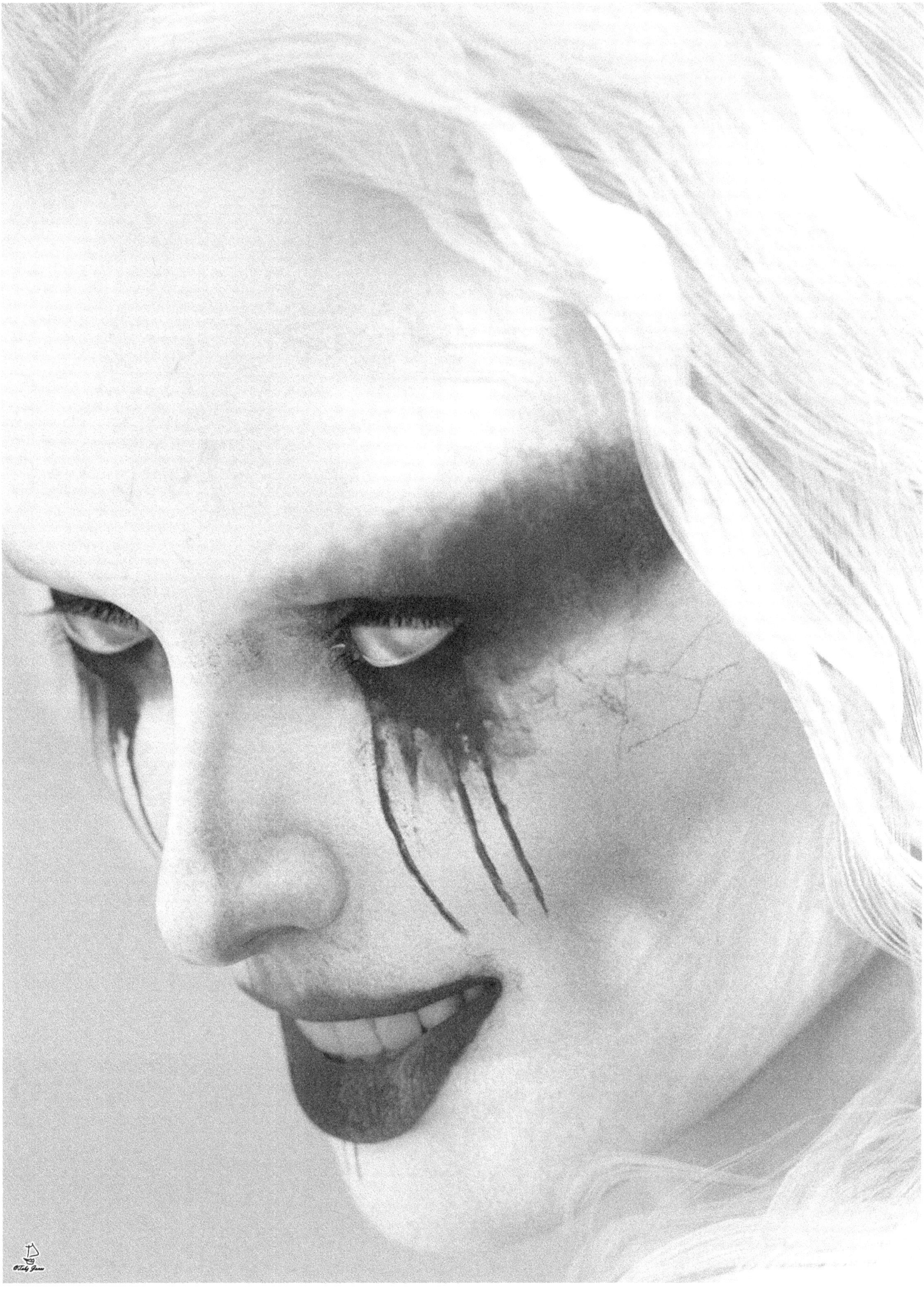

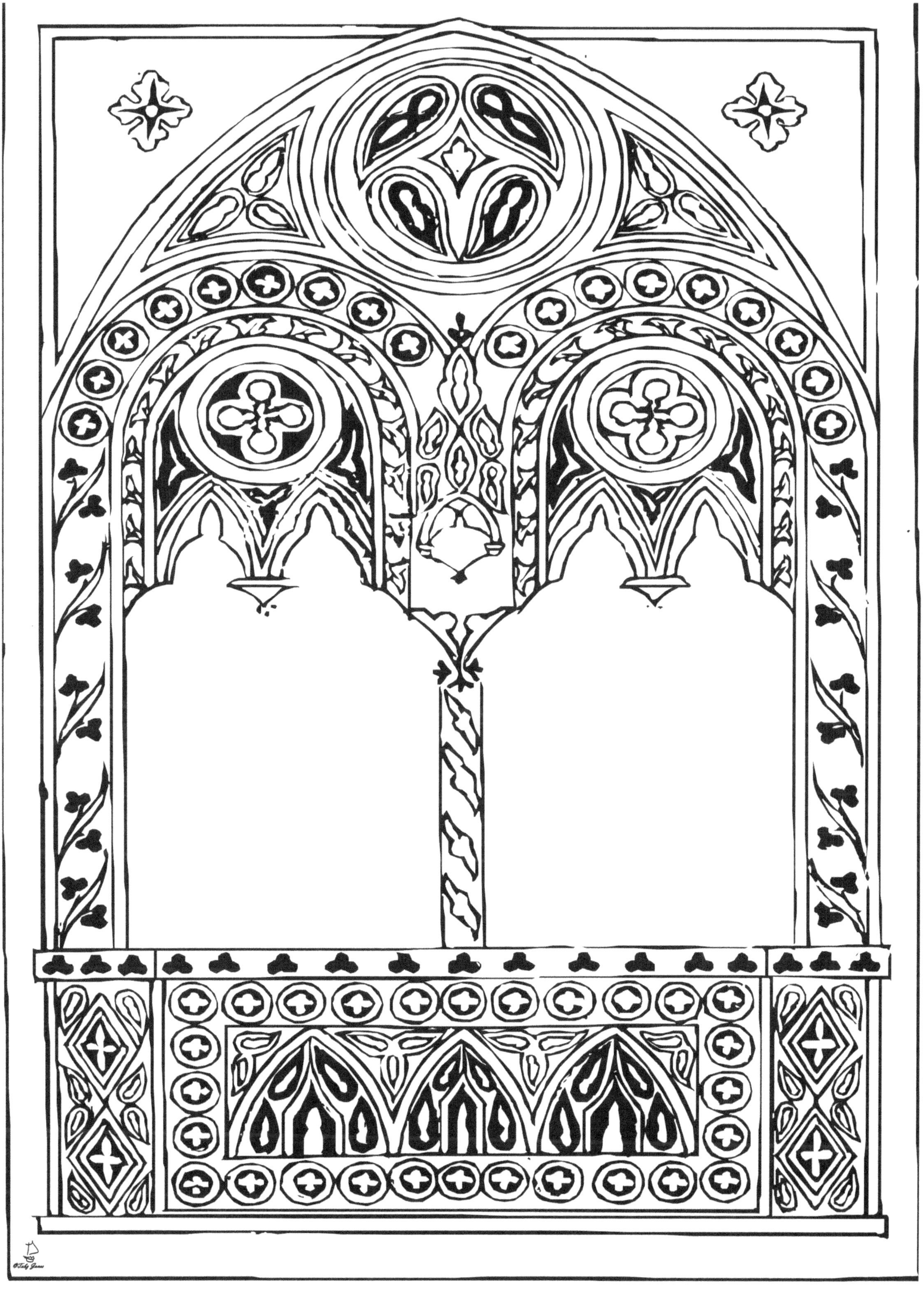

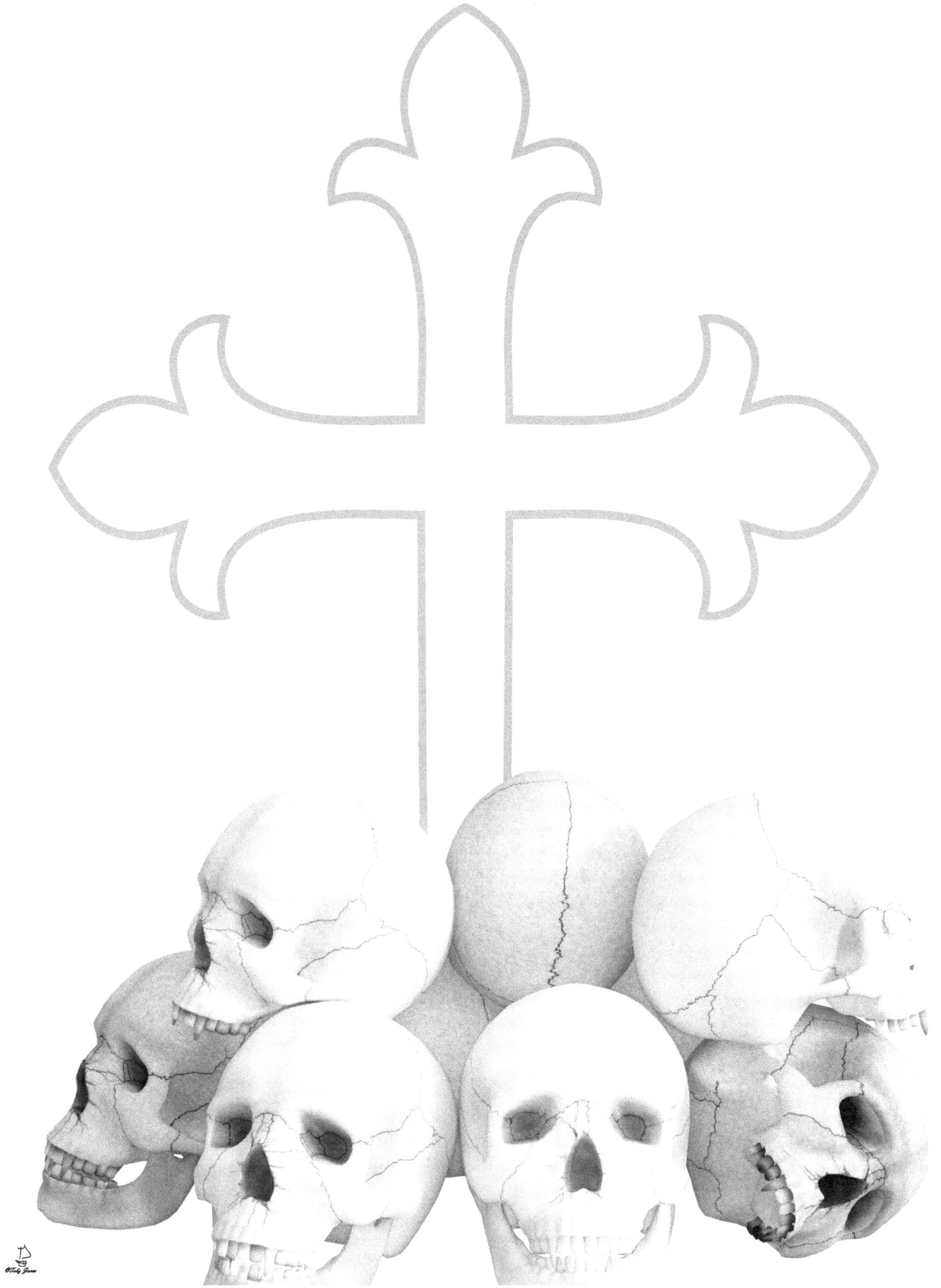

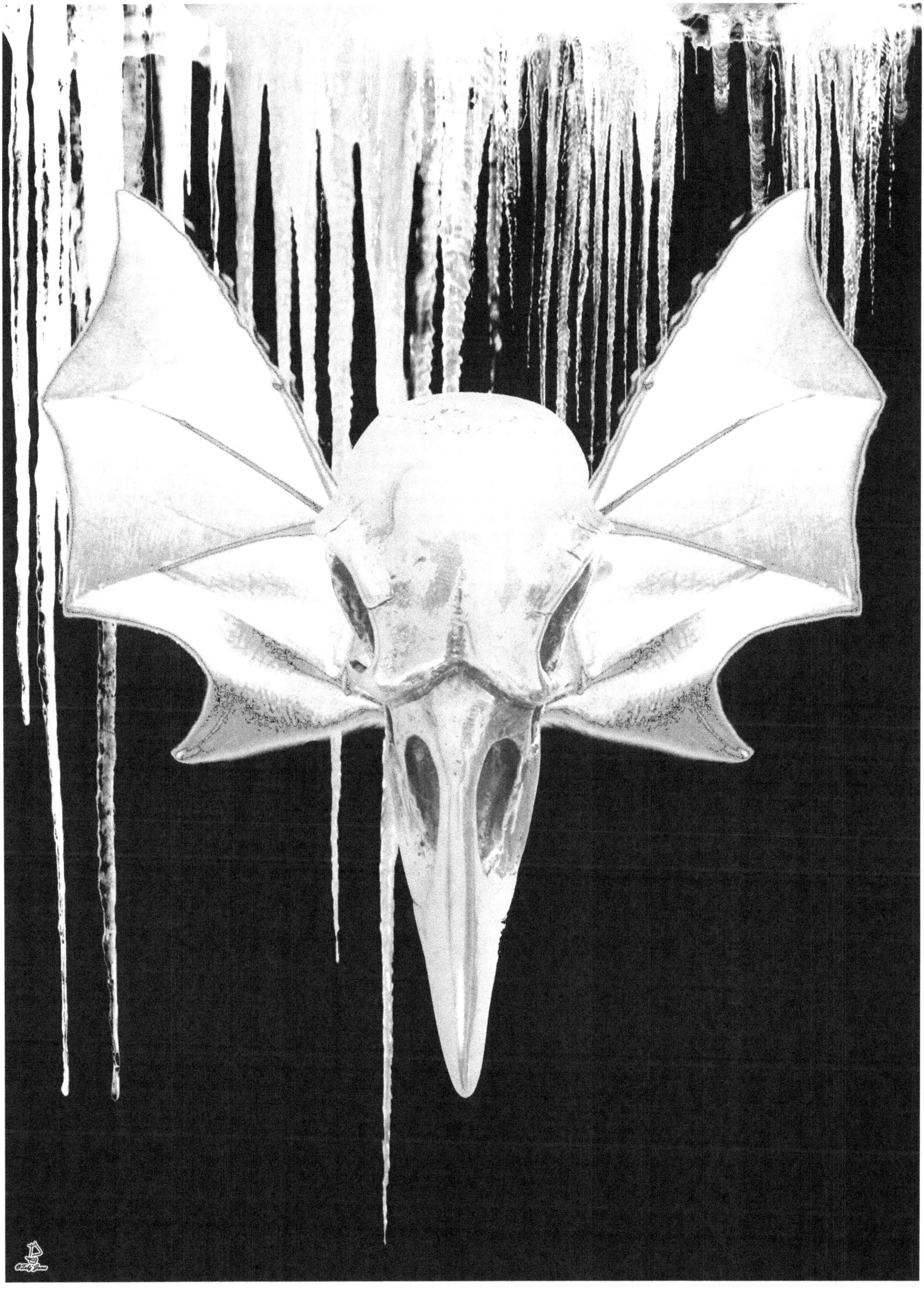

www.ingramcontent.com/pod-product-compliance
Lightning Source LLC
Chambersburg PA
CBHW080138240526
45468CB00009BA/2513

* 9 7 8 1 9 7 3 9 5 1 4 7 6 *